Warning!

Intellectually honest people do not prejudge a book by its cover. From cover to content, this little volume is designed to test the objectivity of the reader who may favor abortion. If the concept of this book has already caused you to suffer pangs of self-righteous disdain, you flunked the objectivity test.

Many before me have compared the holocaust of Germany with present-day abortion. Any such comparison, it is said, is an attempt to elevate emotion above logic. I challenge you to repeat that charge after you have read the book.

This is neither an attempt to resurrect Adolf Hitler, nor an effort to judge sincere

I

people in an unreasonable fashion. If you have made that assumption, again you flunk the objectivity test. On the other hand, the blind pursuit of a false premise led otherwise intelligent people to achieve a comfortable disregard for human life in Germany. And such a philosophy should not be allowed to flourish unchallenged in America.

Multitudes are open-minded on the abortion question, never having been faced with the facts. Facts presented in the form of hard-hitting ideas which demand a reaction are what this book is all about.

Any reader should finish this volume with a clear-cut position on abortion. Is it right or is it wrong? Can you, as a tax-payer, avoid the personal implications of tax-funded abortions? Are we indeed, as a nation, moving toward the thinking we once found so reprehensible in Nazi Germany? When it is all over, feel free to brand me a fool or a prophet - but *please, read the book!*

✦✦✦✦✦✦✦✦✦✦ ABORTION ✦✦✦✦✦✦✦✦✦✦

THE
AMERICAN HOLOCAUST

by
Kent Kelly

III

Library of Congress
Catalog Card Number: 81-65240
International Standard Book Number: 0 9604138-1-2

Order from:
Calvary Press
400 South Bennett Street
Southern Pines, North Carolina 28387

Dedication

To my wife Elizabeth
who gave us both a
personal interest in
the abortion controversy.
(See Chapter 18)

Special Thanks

The production of this book would have been impossible without diligent effort on the part of several people - my secretary, Sissy King, for research, editing, lay-out, and cover design; Sharon Cook for graphics; Lynne Creech, Gerri Taylor, and Bessie Kelly for typing and typesetting.

ABORTION
THE AMERICAN HOLOCAUST

Table of Contents

The Nazi Mentality

"Would you be in favor of abortion if your mother had had one six months before you were born?"

Some questions require no answer. This question demands an answer. It must be asked on behalf of the unborn. Only those who have escaped the threat of this mass murder that is sweeping America have a voice to raise in defense of the helpless in the mother's womb.

This is a handbook suggesting crucial ideas for those who find themselves in debate on this subject. It is also a book designed to challenge the mind of the reader who either favors or has no strong position on abortion. Those who have opportunity to defend the unborn need answers to questions raised by the proponents of abortion. Equally necessary is the clear-cut understanding of the type of

1

thinking which has generated an abortionist climate throughout the nation.

Books abound setting forth the sordid details of abortion methods. Medical doctors have written at length in scholarly terms to supply a mountain of material for those writing a doctoral thesis or other such activity.

This little volume is intended to cut rhetoric to the bone and, in common language, get to the root issues and questions in the abortion controversy. John Q. Public will never labor through pages of documentation. Legislators have no time for extended discussion. Before you are the facts - carefully researched, forcefully stated, ready for use in defense of the most basic of all human rights - the right to life.

The world professes horror at "the Nazi mentality" which, carried to its logical conclusion, ended in the extermination of six million Jews during World War II. Trials for war crimes have since been conducted in an effort to punish some of those responsible. Films, historians, and the media, in general, have portrayed the men in decision-making positions during that era as morally insane villians.

A far greater insanity is to be so morally blind as to relegate "the Nazi mentality" to a certain war, a certain block of history, a certain race, or a certain set of deaths. The crime of the Germans was not that of being Germans. Hatred of Jews or any other race is a social problem of long standing, which has seldom resulted in the murder of six million individuals.

"The Nazi mentality" was a strain of human thought which may be isolated and analyzed in much the same manner as a poisonous toxin which infects the body. "The Nazi mentality" is epitomized in one tangible principle:

"An acceptance of the unwarranted extermination of human beings as a national necessity."

"Nazi" is a scare word to a generation which lived through a World War and experienced the ramifications of fighting a visible, definable enemy. To lift that term out of its historical context, to compare such

3

atrocities with current thinking is nothing short of intellectual heresy to those who live and die by public opinion. Indeed, such tactics might be branded as inflammatory in the extreme.

But, is it not interesting that no one questions the motives or methods of those who point with inflammatory language to the German holocaust? Instead, they are praised as activists for justice and human rights. Our purpose here is to be as inflammatory as possible in pointing to "Abortion - The American Holocaust."

The pro-abortionist feels strongly enough to kill for his or her belief. That is an inflammatory position indeed. Politicians say we should kill for the economic good of our nation. The drain from indigent welfare children makes their extermination a national necessity. The U.S. Supreme Court and the feminists say we should kill for the constitutional good of our nation. The preservation of a woman's rights makes this killing a national necessity. The social engineers say we should kill for the physical and emotional purity of our nation. Unwanted and physically inferior children must be killed as a national necessity.

"The Nazi mentality" is neither dead nor is it exclusive property of the Nazis. In this nation, we long ago surpassed Hitler's six million. Abortions occur in America at an annual rate now surpassing 1,500,000 with no end in sight.

"The Nazi mentality" may still be correctly defined as:

"An acceptance of the unwarranted extermination of human beings as a national necessity."

The Scope of the Holocaust

In our nation's capital Washington, D. C., buried among our "certain inalienable rights", is the right to life. You will find this "self evident" truth written upon the pages of a fading document in the National Archives.

In the Bureau of Statistics in Washington, D. C., you will discover that abortions in that city actually outnumber live births every year. Three abortions for every live birth.

Since the U. S. Supreme Court decision in 1973, over 8 million lives have been destroyed. While such numbers are incomprehensible to the human mind in terms of practical analysis, some comparisons will help us understand the scope of the holocaust.

The number one killer in America is not heart disease - it is abortion.

One out of every four Americans will have cancer at some time in his life. One out of every two Americans is murdered before he has a chance to come into the world.

State and federal governments propagandize us with the tremendous number of lives saved by the 55 mph speed limit each year. At the present rate of lives saved, it would take over 83 years for the reduced speed limit to replace the Americans killed by abortion in 1980.

NOW - the National Organization for Women is the largest feminist group in America supporting abortion on demand. Each year, the number of women killed in their mother's womb is over 5 times the number of women in that organization.

Every 30 seconds around the clock, a baby is murdered by abortion in America.

120 unborn babies are legally murdered by abortion each hour in this nation.

2,880 unborn children are killed each day in America by abortion.

Abortion kills 20,160 babies each week in America.

Each year 1,500,000 children are killed in the womb in the United States.

The equivalent to 10 large hospitals full of children is killed each day.

The equivalent to 540 school bus loads of children is killed each week.

The equivalent to all the Jews in Israel is killed each 18 months.

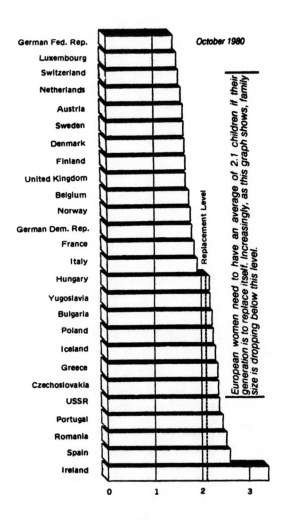

German Fed. Rep.
Luxembourg
Switzerland
Netherlands
Austria
Sweden
Denmark
Finland
United Kingdom
Belgium
Norway
German Dem. Rep.
France
Italy
Hungary
Yugoslavia
Bulgaria
Poland
Iceland
Greece
Czechoslovakia
USSR
Portugal
Romania
Spain
Ireland

October 1980

Replacement Level

European women need to have an average of 2.1 children if their generation is to replace itself. Increasingly, as this graph shows, family size is dropping below this level.

0   1   2   3

10

THE
AMERICAN H🔴L🔴CAUST

**Abortion has taken more American lives than all
the wars in our history, combined.**
(Source: World Book Encyclopedia, 1978 edition)

War	Dates	Americans Killed
Revolutionary War	1775-1782	25,324
War of 1812	1812-1815	2,260
Mexican War	1846-1848	13,288
Civil War	1861-1865	529,332
Spanish-American War	1898-1898	2,446
W.W.I	1914-1918	116,516
W.W.II	1939-1945	405,399
Korea	1950-1953	54,246
Vietnam	1957-1975	56,480
Total American war dead	1775-1975	**1,205,291**
Deaths by abortion		8,000,000

Will your voice and your vote be raised
against this wholesale murder? God has
placed you in a land which has "Government of the people, by the people, and
for the people". The attendant responsibility cannot be ignored.

11

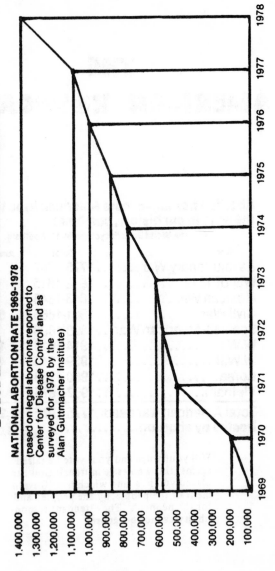

THE
AMERICAN H☀️L☀️CAUST

NATIONAL ABORTION RATE 1969-1978

(based on legal abortions reported to
Center for Disease Control and as
surveyed for 1978 by the
Alan Guttmacher Institute)

12

A lecturer in a well-known medical school asked one of his classes what they would recommend in the following case:

The father had syphillus
The mother had TB
They had four children already:
       l was blind
       l was born dead
       l was a deaf mute
       l had TB,
    The mother was pregnant with her fifth child.

Almost without exception, the medical students indicated that they would recommend abortion.

The lecturer then stated, "Congratulations! You have just killed BEETHOVEN."

★ ★ ★ ★ ★ ★ ★ ★ ★

"If thou forbear to deliver them that are drawn unto death - and those that are ready to be slain: if thou sayest, behold, we knew it not - doth not He that pondereth the heart consider it?"
Proverbs 24:11 & 12

"Therefore to him that knoweth to do good, and doeth it not, to him it is sin."
13   James 4:17

How Did It Happen?

"The destruction process required the cooperation of every sector of German society. The bureaucrats drew the definitions and decrees, the churches gave evidence of Aryan descent . . . A place of execution was made available to the Gestapo by the government. To repeat, the operation required and received the participation of every major social and political and religious institution of the German Reich."

The Cunning of History:
Mass Death and the American Future
Richard L. Rubenstein
Harper & Row, 1975

As illustrated by this comment, the Nazi mentality becomes a pervasive factor in

15

society. Perhaps not so obvious is the development of such a process in America by virtue of the nature of our system.

Liberal churches have long been organized politically. Their political involvement is a direct result of a relatively small group of theologians - always from large urban congregations; always from liberal educational institutions - who perceived their high visibility as an opportunity for social change. Radical thinkers far removed from mainstream Protestantism are at least 45 years ahead of religious conservatives in political involvement.

State councils of churches and the National Council of Churches lobby in the halls of government, in many cases without the slightest awareness on the part of Mr. Average Church Member. Equally relevant is the fact that a majority of theologically conservative Americans is not connected with any state or national council of churches and has no political clout.

A similar circumstance exists in the social realm. Militant feminists do not represent the mainstream of American womanhood, yet their voice, though small, echoes loudly in a room where no other voice is heard. Social activists as a body of lobbying entities have always consisted almost exclusively of the far left.

In government, education is the culprit. Governors who often, themselves, have a humanist educational background must fill appointive positions. These political plums in the bureaucratic hierarchy go to militant activists. Academicians who perceive life as a giant college campus, and who have spent their years becoming educated beyond their intelligence, bring their Nietzsche mentality to human resources. Staff positions for those who research the philosophy to be presented to legislative study groups are filled from the same genre. Given hype by a liberal press, these champions of moral radicalism inform the men in the lawmaking bodies of the glories of "national public policy." The voice of the people becomes the voice of God without explaining that the "voice of the people" consists of a handful of political appointees selected for their rubber-stamp thought patterns. Moral and philosophical diversity cannot be found to any degree among the teams of social planners who bring the pressure on the legislative process.

To summarize, the political efforts of religion in America, the political aspirations of social activists, the political heat of bureaucratic experts, all have been overwhelming in their ability to create mountainous results from molehill support. Supreme Court Justices, as well as legislators, are not immune to public opinion. That "public" has long consisted of a group of pseudo-experts, professing to speak for the public good. A small handful of newspaper editors, educators, social activists, administration lobbyists, and apostate preachers have become the prevailing voice of American public policy.

Should such an hypothesis be true, what about the citizenry? Frederick Wertham, in *A Sign for Cain: An Exploration of Human Violence* (Macmillan, 1969), explains the process in Germany. He states that the prerequisite for holocaust was a gradual surrender of the individual conscience to that of the state. The German populace was not composed of an entire nation of maniacs waiting to destroy their fellows. He says that those who carried out the killings were academic physicians, many times professors in outstanding universities - not insane devotees of Naziism, but pragmatists convinced by the

18

state - that necessity demanded a greater concern for the cost of caring for the elderly than for the cost of killing them.

Those in positions of influence and authority accepted statist principles as unquestionable conclusions of national necessity. Those in the street accepted passive indifference as a way of life by assuming the collective wisdom of those in power to be sufficient justification.

"The American Holocaust" has come to fruition in the same manner. Too many citizens never consider the process by which these decisions are made. The legislator hears the voices of the "experts," the editors, and extremists. He assumes their moral radicalism to be a mandate for legislation reflecting the will of the people. The people assume that representative government has overruled them and settle down to passive indifference as millions of babies are murdered. How did it happen in America? By a chain of events not unlike those in Germany.

Abortion and Humanism

"Humanism" is a term which strikes fear into the hearts of liberals when used in a derogatory sense. They envision the arts and sciences of the humanities crumbling in a rising tide of misinformed public opinion. Consistent with their "humanist" education, they remember the days when apostate Protestant theologians used the term "humanism." In an attempt to accommodate "secular humanism," liberal theologians sought to equate Christian humanism with "humanitarianism." Thus, to be against "humanism" is, in the minds of many, an attack on the Judeo-Christian ethic as it applies to the love of fellow man. If all that sounds confusing, it is.

For the sake of all the humanists who read these pages, our position is relatively simple. We fully understand "humanitarianism" and are in favor of it. In fact, we oppose abortion for "humanitarian" reasons. Second, Bible-believing Christians have never equated "Christian humanism" with "humanitarianism." We totally reject the term "Christian humanism" as a product of apostate theology. All forms of "humanism" are branches of the same tree, as will be discussed momentarily. Third, "the humanities" are legitimate fields of pursuit in our view, so long as the pursuit is Biblically based as opposed to "humanistically" approached.

To summarize:

- "Humanitarianism" is concern for fellow humans.

- "Humanities" are fields of study related to man's activities.

- "Humanistic" is an orientation toward man which may be good or evil.

- "Humanism" is a philosophy of life which is man-centered as opposed to God-centered. 22

- "Humanist" is an adherent to the philosophy of "humanism" in one of its many forms.

The typical "humanist" in American society is often unaware of owning such a title. Many would object adamantly to the term because of the association of the word "humanist" with the official organization of "secular humanism" and its attendant atheism.

For an analogy, there are many categorized as Roman Catholics who do not hold to all the doctrines of Catholicism. Their background is Catholic, their education is Catholic, yet they feel free to pick and choose the elements of Catholicism that they wish to include in their personal philosophy of life. However, with their background and education being Catholic, they may honestly say they are not Catholic only by renouncing Catholicism as a system of beliefs.

Most Americans are "humanists" by background and education. A majority would not admit to such a conclusion for the simple reason that "humanism" is a way of thinking imposed upon the populace without fanfare and without the term "humanism" being

23

used. Way back in 1930, the founder of *The Humanist Society of New York* wrote these telling words:

> "Education is thus a most useful ally of humanism, and every American public school is a school of humanism. What can the theistic (God-centered) Sunday Schools, meeting for an hour once a week, and teaching only a fraction of the children, do to stem the tide of a 5-day program of humanistic (man-centered) teaching?"

"Every American public school is a school of humanism!" So said one of the giants of humanism 50 years ago. Our generation is a humanist generation by background and education, indoctrinated without knowledge that such an undertaking was underway. This is one of the major reasons the pro-abortion mentality is so evident at this hour.

In his book, *The Arrogance of Humanism* (Oxford University Press, 1978), David Ehrenfeld, professor at Rutger's University, said, "No two humanists define humanism the same way." But to define the

24

broad spectrum of belief which identifies a humanist, he used this statement:

> "The humanist temper holds that men should place their faith in man himself - in man's infinite possibilities. This faith should, of course, be coupled with a realistic recognition of man's infinite limitations - of man's capacities for 'sin,' for falling short of the highest he has seen. In a word, faith in intelligence and in man is humanism."

A humanist is one who believes in "secular education" - that man can be educated without God. A humanist is one who believes that in business, in recreation, in government, in the many areas which compose daily life, God has no place. These are the dominions of man where an individual's faith in himself and his own intelligence and ability are paramount. If God is a factor at all in the life of a humanist, he is relegated to Sunday religious observances with a passing prayer or two in time of trouble.

Remember "the arrogance of humanism" - "no two humanists define humanism the same way." How could they when a fundamental of the faith of humanism is that the mind of each individual humanist is the final arbiter of truth?

Remember the statement of the founder of the New York Humanist Society: "Every public school is a school of humanism." It is no wonder at all that John Dewey, *the* leading American educator and first president of the American Humanist Association, spoke often in his writings of "progressive" education as the means of using the schools as instruments of social change.

Humanism has influenced thinking, not only in America, but worldwide. The British Humanist Association has drawn up a 7-point plan for political action. It reads like the brain patterns of the graduating class at the University of North Carolina and is as follows:

- Legalization of homosexuality between consenting adults

- ABORTION ON DEMAND

- Relax   divorce laws

-Legalize voluntary euthanasia

-Legalize "soft drugs"

- Abolition of all forms of censorship

-Abolition of religious education in schools

Every liberal worth the name would subscribe to this 7-point plan for political action - and this is pure unadulterated "humanist" philosophy.

Australian researcher Vince Nesbitt has studied humanism around the world and gives this observation:

"A humanist organization often does not operate as itself. It makes the intellectual bullets for other people to fire. It sets up organizations like the Council for Civil Liberties, the Abortion Law Reform Association, and various other groups to push for political movement in these areas.

"So when you hear a woman cry out for her right to choose...you may not recognize that this is the humanist tenet of selfhood within self-possession. When

27

you know their philosophy, you hear
their slogans."

Humanism is, without question, the
major driving force behind the abortion
movement. A humanist is one who believes
the source of ultimate truth is his own
evaluation of observable facts. He or she is
unmoved by any appeal to God and the Bible
as the source of truth. God must be kept out
of legal decisions and government legislation.
A humanist does not accept the validity of
God in our first document of government as
the One who has endowed us with certain
inalienable rights, such as the right to life.

A humanist education has done its work
to convince the disciples of humanism that
"the separation of church and state" prevents
the GIVER OF LIFE from being a valid
consideration in the right to life.

Confessions of a Humanist

By Sissy Price King

I was a product of many years in a public school, and I don't recall having heard the term "humanist." In retrospect, the absence of the term did nothing to alter the presence of the principles of humanism.

Leaving the public education system of North Carolina, only briefly, to graduate from Northfield School for Girls served to enhance my appreciation for humanism.

There the lovely encircling hills of Massachusetts guarded us every day as we cloistered ourselves for learning and worship. With the same nameless subtlety evident in the public schools of N. C., humanism had

31

crept into Northfield, a school founded by Fundamentalist Evangelist Dwight L. Moody.

I recall passing Moody's birthplace on the way to the bookstore everyday. I recall winding my way through the library's maze of reading rooms with all of Moody's letters and memorabilia on display. Looking back, I also perceive how unheralded were the beliefs, the Bible, and the God of D. L. Moody.

These had been replaced by the finest in humanist education. From religion - philosophy classes devoted to Barth and Niebhur, to frequent instruction from men such as social activist William Sloan Coffin of Yale, our minds soaked up this philosophy as would the minds of all seventeen year-olds hungering after truth.

D. L. Moody's implicit faith in the Word of God as the foundation of all truth had been replaced by the logic of German existentialists, just as the founding fathers' faith had been replaced by the humanism of John Dewey in the public schools of North Carolina. Both systems taught me well.

The goodness of mankind and the good of society were my banners as I returned to

North Carolina to enter Greensboro College. Two more years followed, filled with a study of the humanities as I was in search of a liberal arts education. The word "humanist" had now been neatly catalogued in my mind as one who perpetuated the intellectual value systems of the glory of ancient Greece and Rome.

During this period, I was able to apply my humanism in a practical manner. Traveling to London as a representative of the World Council of Churches and to Botswana, Africa, as a school teacher in a small desert village marked my contributions to religion and the needs of the Third World. Back at college, we had opportunities to put the "situation ethics" principles of our humanist education to work. "Situation ethics" was no longer confined to classroom discussion but blossomed into practice in a co-ed dorm where drinking and drugs were both well hidden and well received.

What could have been more natural or more inevitable than moving on to bigger and better things at East Carolina University in the fall of 1968? After all, I was a religious person being trained in the liberal arts. Drugs, drink, rock concerts, practicing witches, living

33

together in blatant sexual relationships, peace rallies, all were a part of the liberal education for most of the hundreds of fledgling humanists on campus.

I had become what my education assured that I would become, a professional humanist with a liberal education and a totally distorted view of reality.

In these days before the U.S. Supreme Court approved abortion on demand, we had other means. It never occurred to me to question my friends at East Carolina University who performed abortions for needy students. We had learned our situation ethics well. I considered their efforts to be helpful. It would surely save emotional pain for one finding herself pregnant in the age of the pill. Drugs, drinking, and cohabitation were the norm.

The question is not - "Why did I think this way?" - but rather - "How could I have possibly thought any other way in view of my education?"

I ended my public education career with a piece of paper certifying that I had obtained a Bachelor of Fine Arts degree. A more honest document would have called it a degree in humanism. After 17 years of education, I left school with my idealism and a husband who had also obtained a Masters Degree in Humanism. We set out on a totally useless and unproductive life to be artists in an unappreciative world. We made a pilgrimage to Maine to live out a fantasy as harbingers of truth and good - a blessing to society.

In 1972 I set out on another journey, a journey from faith in human potential and the goodness of man to faith in the Saviour of sinners. I became a *former* humanist! After years filled with education, money, religion, travel opportunities, and confidence in the goodness of mankind, I considered the true message of the Bible. "There is none good, no not one." "What shall it profit a man if he shall gain the whole world and lose his own soul?"

When I examined the failures of the systems of accumulated knowledge, when I learned from experience that we humans are sinners by nature, by choice and by practice - I was more than ready as the Lord Jesus Christ presented Himself to my mind and heart as "The *Way*, the *Truth*, and the *Life*."

Realizing fully for the first time that He died on the cross as my substitute, I trusted in His finished work as my only hope for eternal life. The school founded by D. L. Moody has long since forsaken the truth of the Word of God and turned to humanism. The Methodist Church of my youth and the World Council of Churches I served have gone into apostasy. The public schools of this nation teach a secular religion - the religion of humanism rooted in faith in man.

As a former humanist, I understand more each day how pervasive had been my anti-Christian training. How thoroughly my thoughts were directed by the education I received. Only a mind twisted and perverted by humanism could have accepted the murder of little babies on the college campus or elsewhere, as a necessity of life in a rational society.

I am now in 1981, a humanist turned Christian school teacher. Can that really be possible? Only by becoming what the Lord has promised to make all who come to Him - "A new creature in Christ Jesus."

The Humanist Gestapo

In drawing the unmistakable parallels between Hitler's holocaust and "Abortion - The American Holocaust," we must not forget the Humanist Gestapo.

As stated previously, "the Nazi mentality" is an acceptance of the *unwarranted extermination of human beings as a national necessity.* Such was the general mood of the times which allowed the atrocities to come to fruition. However, at the heart of the movement was an inner circle of dedicated storm troopers. The very mention of the word "Gestapo" - even in a whisper - caused strong men to tremble. The philosophy of the Gestapo went beyond "an acceptance of the unwarranted extermination of human beings as a national necessity." To these individuals, the key word was not "acceptance," but rather, "advocacy." Mass murder was not simply an unpleasant necessity to the Gestapo - it was a cause to be pursued with zeal and dedication. Extermination could "purify the race," "increase the dignity of the masses," "eliminate the unwanted and the weak." Such are the battle cries of "the Humanist Gestapo" in the American Holocaust.

Not only is "the Humanist Gestapo" to be found among the rank and file, they are most prevalent in positions of influence in state and federal governments. These positions of influence have been achieved by demonstrating uncommon dedication to the philosophy of social science.

The Department of Human Resources, by its very name, reflects the hypothesis that human beings are "resources" of the state which must be used to best advantage. Just as the Department of "Natural" Resources oversees the trees and water for the good of society, someone must do extensive social planning to see that the "human resources" are channeled in the right direction. All this seems logical and necessary until we ask who determines what will ultimately be "the right direction."

Frederic Bastiat, in his classic little book *The Law* summarized, in the last century, the proper function of government. He said that the purpose of law is "to protect life, liberty, and property." In this nation, founded upon the premise that we have "a government of laws and not of men," we have gone far afield.

Government, having ventured into the business of social planning, must of necessity look to its "experts" for guidance when formulating law. Standing in the wings with bated breath, waiting for a legislative hearing on tax-funded abortion, we find "the Humanist Gestapo." With tear in eye and appropriation request in hand they tell of unwanted children, coat hanger abortions, child abuse, and the need to increase their bloated salaries to protect our human resources. Their expertise consists of a misguided zeal, a secular humanist education, and a desire to eliminate lives with the tax money of those who are solidly against their position.

Call a Tail a Leg

Abe Lincoln once asked a man, "How many legs would a sheep have if you called his tail a leg?" The man replied, "Five." Lincoln said, "No, the sheep would still have only four legs because no matter how often you call a tail a leg it never becomes one."

Semantics played a tremendous role in the Jewish holocaust. Mass murder was called "defending the nation." Mass murder was called "obeying orders in accord with military procedure." Semantics also provide the justification for "the American Holocaust."

On January 22, 1973, the U.S. Supreme Court ruled that during the first six months of life an unborn child is denied legal status under the U.S. Constitution. They stated that the child is the property of the mother and may be destroyed at will. The Court further ruled upon the status of life before birth by allowing the murder of the baby *at any time* during the nine months of pregnancy with medical approval. One licensed physician may approve an abortion. His reason need only be a superficial opinion that the birth of the child would damage the mother's physical or mental health. The determination of a threat to her mental health may include either "social or economic" distress.

The U.S. Supreme Court in *Roe v. Wade,* 410 U.S. 113 (1973) and *Doe v. Bolton,* 410 U.S. 179 (1973), for all intents and purposes, legitimatized abortion on demand. In so doing they used such terms as "viability" and "the potentiality of human life." Such weak attempts to "call a tail a leg" do not for one moment negate the facts of science or the fact, duly noted in the founding of this nation, that God is the Author, Creator, and Bestower of the rights to life, liberty, and the pursuit of happiness.

A ten-week old baby resting comfortably in a mother's womb is not a "potential" human being. The "viability" of that life is proved by its very existence, unless some murderous human intervention interrupts the process which brought even the U.S. Supreme Court Justices into the world.

The Court refused to touch the question of when life begins, but clearly approved the undeniably religious belief that life does not begin at conception. Such a conclusion is drawn from faith in the evolutionary process, as well as a decidely antagonistic view toward the Biblical concept of life.

Certainly it is ironic that the U.S. Supreme Court, guardian of the U.S. Constitution and its progenitor, the Declaration of Independence, should be the means of destroying the most basic of rights.

"We hold these truths to be self-evident: That all men are created equal in the third trimester. That they are endowed by the evolutionary process with certain inalienable rights depending on their viability as a human being. That among these are the right to death so long as it occurs before the deadline; liberty, if the the mother and physician agree; and the

pursuit of happiness should they not be one of the victims of "Abortion - 'The American Holocaust.'"

This new Declaration of Independence, written in blood by the U.S. Supreme Court, does not alter the facts. A tail is not a leg because some thoughtless observer declares it so. And an aborted baby is still a murdered human being in spite of the fact that the U.S. Supreme Court designates it a "potential life."

Abortion Politics

Inevitably, the question arises, "Haven't you people ever heard of the separation of church and state? What right do you have to impose your morality on society?"

The answer should be in the form of a challenge. "What right do you have to impose your morality on us?" Somehow the humanists have managed to intimidate those who should be intimidating. The Johnny-come-lately philosophy around here is abortion on demand. Countless generations of rational human beings testify to the validity of our position.

Since when are you disenfranchised as a citizen because you believe the Bible?

49

Abortion is a moral issue. Laws and government agencies will validate and practice someone's views of abortion. Free speech is in full swing when humanists editoralize in major newspapers to express their decidedly religious belief on the moral issue known as abortion.

Some people believe in abortion. Some people do not. The only remaining question is - whose beliefs will prevail? It is the height of hypocrisy to suggest that it is somehow un-American to transgress the anti-Christian precepts of a Supreme Court which has denied our history. Yet, all is well when we transgress the precepts of the Word of God.

Be that as it may, every newspaper editor, every lobbyist, every feminist, every bureaucrat, is striving for legislation on the basis of his personal beliefs. Where they get those beliefs is immaterial. Perhaps their views come from their church, their education, or their pet parrot; but under any circumstances, the beliefs they hold are no more valid than yours.

The fact that I walk through a church door, another walks through a door in the Department of Human Resources, and another walks through the door of the editorial offices of a newspaper enroute to speak and lobby on the abortion question has no bearing on the subject. Tragically, many walk through church doors on the way to lobby in favor of tax-funded abortion.

As long as free speech remains a constitutional right in America, every citizen who believes in the anti-abortion stance held by this nation for generations has a responsibility to challenge advocates of abortion. The historical legal, ethical, and moral concensus of 200 years must not be brushed aside by the social demagogues who accuse us of demagoguery.

Politics in a land purported to have "a government of laws and not of men" is a process of lawmaking and law enforcement. The law of the land touches many facets of life. Any area touched by law becomes political by its very nature.

Tax-exempt status for churches has never been considered a form of "subsidy" until modern times. Modern times being the past two decades in which we have seen the Infernal Revenue Service appoint itself an instrument of social change. By regulations and interpretations, a full-scale effort is underway to circumvent the U.S. Congress, rewrite American history, and bring all Christian institutions under the hobnail boot of the Internal Revenue Service.

Tax-exempt status is not and never has been a form of aid to churches, as it is to all the myriad of tax-exempt organizations in other realms. The church has historically been exempt because government derives from God - not God from government. To levy tax has become a way of life by presuming that every institution "owes" something to the state by virtue of its existence. The church, as God's representative in the world, is not a local affiliate of "The Furry Friends Humane Society" and may not be treated as such.

Much rhetoric is being circulated by those who are self-styled guardians of the American conscience. They see their beliefs as worthy of note in the halls of Congress while opposing any beliefs held by "religious" folks as invalid. The fear seems to be that America will be destroyed by preachers taking over the government.

Experience and reason dictate that the hope of the nation is freedom of expression coupled with representative government. We must remind these people that preachers *have* taken over the government. Men preaching a certain set of beliefs always get elected. An appeal to God and the Bible as the source of morality in matters such as abortion is only intimidating to those who reject God and the Bible. We fear a takeover by those who preach the fundamentals of the Humanist faith. They fear a takeover by those who preach the fundamentals of the Christian faith. In the final analysis a takeover of any segment of government by either group is impossible so long as the Constitution stands and citizens live up to their political obligations.

The very people who will vociferously attack the premise of this book and its inquiry into "the Nazi mentality" are those who have compared us in the media to the Nazis, the Klan, and the Iranian religious leaders. We must remind them that our brand of "Naziism" does not advocate "the unwarranted extermination of human beings as a national necessity."

Some of the most arrogant, narrow-minded bigotry you will ever encounter comes from the "broad-minded" liberals who pride themselves in their openness to the free exchange of ideas.

Rather than meet in head to head debate, the tactic is to catagorize our position as one of ignorance at worst and anti-intellectualism at best.

The time has come to meet that type of dishonesty with a challenge. Where is the historical concensus for the present disregard for human life? Excluding arbitrary labels, why are our beliefs any more the product of personal faith than theirs? Why should the church be silent when the Civil Liberties Union speaks? Why should anyone be silent as long as freedom of speech remains in the Bill of Rights? As the other chapters of this book explain - totally apart from the Bible and Religion - where is the logic for the pro-abortion position?

Legislators Beware!

A Senator or Representative sits in the hottest seat of all on the matter of abortion. The mindless few look to those who control them politically and vote accordingly. The vast majority will vote one of two ways on any issue - either conscience or the will of the people.

In the summer of 1980, a New York Times/CBS News poll reached the following profound conclusion:

QUESTION
"Do you think there should be an amendment to the Constitution prohibiting abortions, or shouldn't there be such an amendment?"

RESULTS
62% - No   29% - Yes   9% - Unsure

After posing this question to a random sample of Americans, they then rephrased the question to the same group as follows:

QUESTION
"Do you believe there should be an amendment to the Constitution protecting the life of the unborn child, or shouldn't there be such an amendment?"

RESULTS
50% - Yes   39% - No   11% - Unsure

While many would interpret this poll as concluding nothing more than voter vacillation, an astute politician can look behind the scenes. The world of a legislator is one of bi-lingual confusion. The folks in the Capital speak a language known as "bureaucratese." As a new legislator comes to work for the first time, he or she is faced with learning the language and customs of a foreign culture.

The key to success is remembering that the folks back home react to gut issues. All the subtleties of study commission reports,

58

testimony by administration lobbyists, etc., etc., fall by the wayside when the subject is dead babies. Senator Birch Bayh was outraged at being called a "baby-killer" by his opposition. Outraged or not - he lost!

The wise politician understands the folks back home to this degree - semantics reign supreme. "Prohibiting abortions" - "Protecting the life of the unborn child." What's the difference? Twelve percentage points. More than enough to win or lose any election. The folks back home do not "terminate" crabgrass in the lawn - they kill it! They eventually conclude that a "drug abuser" is in fact a "dope addict." Sooner or later, they become aware that when the Department of Human Resources speaks of "birth control methods," among other things, they mean killing babies.

Many legislators make TV spots and political speeches to say, "I supported a balanced budget." What they mean is, "When the time came to vote on a bill I pushed the button." Nothing more - nothing less. No action under consideration may come to fruition without sufficient votes. The votes not only permit, but *cause* the action. Birch Bayh to the contrary, a legislator who votes to buy school buses is the *cause* of school buses being bought. A legislator who votes to fund abortion is the *cause* of babies being killed. Buses would never be bought and babies would never be killed without sufficient votes.

Each legislator who votes in favor of tax-funded abortion bears a personal responsibility for each baby put to death with that money.

There can be no doubt about the fact that the sentiments of pro-abortionist bureaucrats do not reflect the views of the average voter when the semantics are stripped away.

The Christian and Abortion

Most of this volume is directed toward reason for a specific purpose. Pro-abortionists across the entire spectrum have little or no regard for the Bible and its implications for the question at hand. Those few who claim that the Bible supports their position are definitely the product of apostate theology.

Bible believing Christians who read these pages should be aware of several facts. We face two separate and distinct problems. Apathy in the church allows abortion to sweep the nation. Our mission, as informed and concerned Christians, is to acquaint our friends and associates with the scope of the problem. An appeal must be made through biblical principles to educate and motivate enroute to a solution.

On the other hand, to sit in our churches and agree to abhor abortion is nothing less than hypocrisy. Our message to the nation must be communicated in a practical manner or no change will be forthcoming. Approaching the world at large with Bible in hand is an exercise in futility. To them, such methodology is no more effective than someone coming to you with a copy of the Koran to prove a point.

My suggestion is not that we abandon the Bible in favor of carnal reason. Instead, we must take the wisdom gained from the Word of God and apply it to the real world. The real world for most people is a world of practical atheism.

Those who understand the nature of the Bible are fully aware that God has spoken, at least in principle, to every conceivable question of life. Humanists reject that notion under the banner of theological disagreement. They would tell us, and correctly so, that others who claim the Bible as their authority take an opposite view. For this reason, some concession must be made to their lack of understanding of religious liberalism and apostasy.

Truth is it s own defense. The Lord said, "Wisdom is justified of her children." We have history on our side. We have public concensus on our side. We have medical and scientific facts on our side. We have logic on our side. Humanists do not acknowledge that history, public concensus, scientific facts, and logic all have religious overtones. Not perceiving their humanism to be a religion based on personal faith, the humanists seek to avoid religion as a topic of discussion. Typically, the humanist would say - "I have my religion and you have yours, but we disagree so let's not make abortion a religious issue."

Our response will determine our ability to be heard. We need not give them the ammunition they seek with which to shoot our arguments. If they can relegate us to some isolated corner of the theological world by slander and innuendo, they will do so. If, on the other hand, we meet them on their own ground we will get results.

Humanists are not afraid of history, public concensus, science, and logic. They see these as the domain of man where God has

65

little impact. In speaking to media, in public debate, as we write to newspapers and lobby the lawmakers, we need not appeal to faith in the Word of God. American history says that "We are endowed by our Creator with certain inalienable rights, that among these are . . . the right to life." Public concensus says that voters are against the use of tax money to murder babies before they have a chance to experience life in the world. Science says that there is no point after conception at which it may be said life does not exist. Logic says it is wrong to accept the unwarranted extermination of human beings as a national necessity.

This book is designed to give you ideas which defeat the humanists on their own battlegrounds. God says abortion is wrong. But to lead with that statement is to play into the hands of those who would negate sound argument by pseudo-intellectual hatchet jobs on the source of our reasoning. Far better to say - history is against abortion, public conscensus, science, and logic all militate against abortion - and last but by no means least - God is against abortion. Force people to fight the facts before they begin to fight the faith.

An
Atheist
Jew?

Dr. Bernard Nathanson describes himself as a Jewish atheist. Such are his qualifications for not being categorized as a Bible-thumping fundamentalist. Dr. Nathanson is an expert. Once a member of "the Humanist Gestapo," he is now a convert. Not a convert to Christianity, but a convert to rejecting wholesale abortion.

Dr. Bernard Nathanson has personally presided over 75,000 abortions as both a physician and an administrator. He was the director of the world's largest abortion clinic. As a board-certified obstetrician-gynecologist, a fellow of the American College of Obstetricians and Gynecologists, and the American College of Surgeons, he just may qualify as having some knowledge of the abortion issue. In 1969, Dr. Nathanson was co-founder of the National Association for the Repeal of Abortion Laws and was responsible, more than any other single person, for the repeal of the abortion laws in New York State, which many believe led to the 1973 decisions by the U.S. Supreme Court.

Dr. Nathanson has written a book entitled *Aborting America* (Doubleday, 1979), which should be read by every proponent of abortion. While he discounts the Biblical arguments of people such as myself, with absolutely no religious considerations whatsoever he explodes the myriad of myths which led him to be a general in "the Humanist Gestapo." Of course he does not use that term, seeing himself only as a misguided, misinformed zealot - but the conclusions are the same.

The Expert Speaks

Dr. Nathanson says that those who classify a fetus as "mere tissue" are using a line of argumentation which is "biological nonsense, unworthy of the people who have advocated it." Dr. Nathanson attacks the "woman and her doctor" theory - the view that they alone should decide on abortion. He quotes another author who says, "Abortion is no more a medical issue because doctors do it than is capital punishment a matter of electrical engineering because an electric chair is used."

Dr. Nathanson speaks of the "unwanted child" syndrome. He says, "If anything, the statistical reports would lead one to conclude that liberal abortion laws, not strict ones, foster child abuse . . . Child abuse has risen noticeably since abortion was legalized, and so have illegitimate births, despite the availability of abortion as an alternative . . . If a fetus is carried to term it will be 'unwanted' only for the nine months between conception and birth. It need never be 'unwanted' because of the hopeless shortage of babies available for the long list of childless couples who earnestly want to adopt them."

Dr. Nathanson speaks of "the coat hanger" argument. He admits that back-alley abortion was one of his early motivations in the pro-abortion cause. Don't miss his comments here. "In the movement we generally emphasized the drama of the individual case, not the mass statistics; but when we spoke of the latter, it was always '5000 to 10,000 deaths a year.' I confess that I knew the figures were totally false, and I suppose the others did too if they stopped to think of it. But in the 'morality' of our revolution, it was a useful figure, widely accepted, so why go out of our way to correct it with honest statistics?" Dr. Nathanson then states the corrected figures. He says that in 1967 before abortion was legalized, the federal government listed only 160 deaths from illegal abortion. In 1972, the last year before the U.S. Supreme Court decision opened the abortion door, there was a total of 39 deaths from illegal abortions. Certainly, even 39 women are important among the tens of millions in America. But it is absolute insanity - even for the guardians of our "human resources" - to shout for the lives of 39 women in 1972 and say nothing of the lives of 1,500,000 babies murdered in 1980.

Dr. Nathanson speaks to the issue of "cost benefit." He refers to the view championed by Washington that it is cheaper for society to destroy babies at $100 apiece by abortion than to take responsibility for aiding poor women and children. He says, "Are we supposed to consider such pragmatism of fetus elimination to be liberal and humanitarian? ... This may be good politics but it is hardly exemplary social morality. It reeks of the Pentagon's 'body count' thinking of the Viet Nam era. Certain human issues are too grave to be handled in this way and must be shielded from a cost-effectiveness theory. Abortion is one of them."

Such are the expert views of Dr. Bernard Nathanson, M.D., former director of the world's largest abortion clinic, founder of the most effective pro-abortion movement in America, supervisor of the deaths of 75,000 human beings - but a Jew who personally managed to escape the holocaust. Not the one in Germany - "Abortion - The American Holocaust."

In fairness to Dr. Nathanson, he rejects any analogy between German genocide and American fetuscide. But I say again - we cannot escape the conclusion that:

> **"an acceptance of the unwarranted extermination of human beings as a national necessity"**

is not uniquely evil because it is mixed with racism. If anything, such thinking is worse when no racism is involved. The racist may be a fool for his bigotry and murderous intentions. But what of the mind which can accept the unwarranted extermination of human beings with no strong feelings of any kind?

Voices
of
Reason

Dr. Bernard Nathanson could hardly be surpassed in expert testimony, but he is not alone. "The Humanist Gestapo" likes to promulgate a thesis of bigotry in their zeal for the cause. "Red-neck fundamentalists, right-to-life Romanists, religious anti-intellectuals of all varieties seek to impose their morality upon us. It's us against them." Such are the tactics of many in the American Holocaust.

Abortion is a religious issue only to those who believe the Bible. Morality or immorality means nothing to dead babies. The all-encompassing question is whether Dr. Bernard Nathanson has a right to live and grow up to become a self-styled "Jewish

77

atheist." The Bible teaches that he does if he pays the eternal consequences of such a belief. Common sense, the founding principles of America, science - men and women have many reasons for rejecting abortion and, in particular, tax-funded abortion.

Arguments raised by purveyors of the American Holocaust are refuted on every hand. Only a few will be cited here as examples:

UNWANTED CHILDREN

"An unwanted pregnancy in the early months does not necessarily mean an unwanted baby after delivery. Dr. Edward Lenoski of the University of California has conclusively shown that 90% of battered children were planned pregnancies."

Willke, Handbook on Abortion
Hayes Publishing Company

RAPE

"Although frequently cited by pro-abortionists, pregnancies resulting from rape are so rare as to be virtually non-existent. There are several contributing factors to this. In addition to the pure mathematical odds against pregnancy resulting from a single random act, medical research indicates that an extremely high precentage of women exposed to severe emotional trauma will not ovulate. The rape itself, therefore acts as a psychological 'birth control.' "

"Indications for Induced Abortion"
F.D. Mecklenburg, M.D.
New York, 1972

RAPE

"A scientific study of 1,000 cases of rape treated medically right after the rape resulted in zero cases of pregnancy."
J. Kuchera
Journal of the
American Medical Association
October 25, 1971

HANDICAPPED CHILDREN

"Though it may be both common and fashionable to believe that the malformed enjoys life less than normal, this appears

to lack both empirical and theoretical
support."   D. Van Hoeck
Address
American Psychological
Association Meeting, 1971

REDUCING DISEASE

"Talk about breeding out genetic diseases
is a lot of nonsense. Seriously affected
persons are unlikely to marry and have
children; the genes are passed along by
carriers. For instance, there are 40
carriers for every person with sickle cell
anemia."

"If every victim of this disease were
eliminated, it would require 750 years
just to cut the incidence in half; to stamp
it out altogether would require 200,000
abortions for every 500,000 couples.
Because each 'normal' person is the
carrier of three or four bad genes, the
only way to eliminate genetic diseases
would be to sterilize or abort
everybody."

Dr. Hymie Gordon
Chairman of the
Dept. of Medical Genetics
Mayo Clinic, Minnesota

80

BIRTH CONTROL

"Our abortion statistics show that people are choosing this as a major form of birth control. That to me, as a physician and a person, *is barbaric.* The major tragedy is that it is the affluent and middle class people who are looking to abortion as a birth control method."

Dr. Lewis L. Bock
Chief of the Personal Health Section
State Division of Health Services
Raleigh, N. C.

TAX-FUNDED ABORTIONS

"I am against the use of my taxes for abortions. This reminds me too much of Nazi Germany where the state was permitted to decide who would live and who must die. I can't be a partner to killing innocent lives."

Francis X. Berry, M.D.
Obstetrician/Gynecologist
Greensboro, N. C.

IMPOSED MORALITY

"One of the fundamental reasons the U.S. Supreme Court has allowed abortion was

81

their belief that anti-abortionists should not be able to impose their morality upon the nation. If that argument has any validity, then it is equally true that pro-abortionists should not be able to impose their wish to fund elective abortions upon the people who oppose such funding."

Dennis L. Cuddy., Ph.D.
Raleigh, N. C.

MORALITY OF ABORTION

"One must understand the value God places on the life of the fetus. Exodus 21:22 & 23 is clear. The unborn child deserves the same protection as any other created being. 'If men strive, and hurt a woman with child, so that her fruit depart from her, and yet no mischief follow; he shall be surely punished, according as the woman's husband will lay upon him; and he shall pay as the judges determine. And if any mischief follow, then thou shalt give life for life.'

"The word used in the phrase, ' . . . so that her fruit depart,' is not the Hebrew word used for miscarriage; it is the word used for delivering the child. In this verse, the inference is a premature delivery. In such a case, the one who caused the trouble is fined as the husband and judges determine. But if the child is killed ('if any mischief follow'), God demands a 'life for a life.' The punishment is the same as that punishment executed for murder of a child after it is born."

William Billings
ALERT
Washington, D. C.

SOCIAL NEED

"When doctors are willing to become social executioners for millions of babies, we must examine what motives are used to justify their actions. Usually, reasons given include preserving the life of the mother, the expectation of a defective child, rape, and incest. Even if these were valid reasons, they would account for only 3% of all abortions. A full 97% of abortions occur for matters of convenience and economy."

C. Everett Koop, M.D.
Surgeon-in-Chief
Childrens Hospital of Philadelphia
From "Abortion in America"

WHEN LIFE BEGINS

"The majority of our group (one dissent out of 60 participants) could find no point in time between the union of sperm and egg and the birth of the infant, at which point we could say that this was not a human life."

First International Conference
on Abortion
(Composed of world-renowned
geneticists, biochemists, physicians,
professors, research scientists, etc.)
Washington, D. C. (1967)

The Brink of Insanity

Arguments in favor of abortion must be dealt with in speaking to legislators and the media. One reporter recently asked, "Something I have never been able to understand is this. Why is it that you people are against abortion and favor the death penalty, while the other side favors abortion and is against the death penalty?"

My answer is very simple. We believe the Bible. The Bible is against abortion and favors the death penalty. God seeks to preserve the lives of the innocent and to take away the lives of those who take the lives of others. As for those who take the opposite view, their position borders on the brink of insanity. What possible logic could be involved in fighting to take the lives of the innocent while fighting to preserve the lives of the guilty?

One of the best approaches to discussion of pro-abortion justifications is to point out such illogical flaws in other areas.

Abortion Saves the Taxpayers Money

Indeed, this is true. But is it sound reasoning? Aborted babies at least stand a chance of becoming productive members of society. One child who adds to the welfare rolls for a few years, but eventually becomes a millionaire businessman, will contribute enough tax money in his lifetime to offset the poverty of many.

If it is reasonable to kill people to save the taxpayer s money, why not begin with prisoners who have long sentences and cost society an average of $9000 per year during their incarceration? Why not kill everyone over 25 who is on welfare? Or everyone on social security or Medicaid? These are all proven offenders, guilty of the crime of costing the taxpayers money. If it is right and reasonable to kill to save money, we should demand to know why the advocates of such reasoning are not prepared to begin with the handicapped, the aged, the prisoners, the retarded, the insane, etc. How is it logical to single out those who may one day pay their own way and ignore those who are a permanent drain on society?

Abortion Represents
A Woman's Right to Choose

In many circles, feminists rally to the pro-abortion cause as another expression of women's rights. This, again, is an argument from the brink of insanity. If the true cause is the glory of womanhood, why is it *selective* women's rights instead of protecting all women equally? Since the Supreme Court abortion decision in 1973, an average of 80,000 women in each of the 50 states will never have the right to choose anything. That many female babies have been murdered in their mother s wombs. Eighty thousand militant feminists in each state in the Union could rock the political world on any subject. However, the truth of the matter is that if all those little ladies could be brought back to life, they would not support abortion as representing a woman's right to choose.

A Majority of Americans Favor Abortion

This is debatable, but suppose it is true. America was never intended to be a nation of majority rule as a blanket premise. A lynch mob is majority rule. The elimination of certain people for the good of society is not the prerogative of any man, woman, group, doctor, judge, or any combination thereof, without a trial and presentation of evidence against the accused. If the right to life may be eliminated on the basis of public sentiment, then any other right may be taken away by majority decision. No right is more basic. No right is more obvious. Only someone on the brink of insanity would want his right to live put to a vote of the majority.

Abortion Prevents
The Tragedy of Unwanted Children

Two factors are often cited in this line of argument. One is the child a family cannot afford. The other is the child who is unloved. Again, it is impossible to refute the statement as it stands. Abortion does indeed prevent the tragedy of unwanted children and children their parents cannot afford. But what of the logic involved? If extermination of such potentially troublesome children while they are still in the womb is right, why begin there? Why not send doctors and psychologists from house to house to administer death-dealing injections as they see fit? If it is a greater tragedy to be poor and unwanted than to be dead, we have much work to do on the present population. A child in the womb is not conscious of being poor or unwanted. Hundreds of thousands of children living outside the womb are feeling the effects of these conditions every day. Surely, the reasonable course of action would be to begin with actual suffering instead of potential suffering. Of course, it is true that these suffering children have lived outside the womb for a while, but what possible difference could a few months make if the true tragedy is to be poor or unwanted? It should make no difference to those whose reasoning is on the brink of insanity.

Save My Wife!

The most emotional of all approaches to the abortion question is that of "either/or" survival.

For a psychological foot-in-the-door, those who advocate abortion say, "Surely you Bible-toters accept abortion when the woman's life is in danger." Many Christians fall into this trap and justifiably lose the whole foundation of their argument. The pro-abortionist moves in for the kill. "If the issue is right-to-life, who has a right to live? Why is the mother more important? If God determines destiny and He chooses to have the child live and the mother die, who are you to intervene?"

All of these are valid questions. The simple fact is that we either trust the Lord to do what is best or we do not. As a Christian, you have no business debating the abortion issue unless you are against abortion, period. Of course religious arguments hold no water for pro-abortionists.

We need an answer for those who raise the "save my wife" flag, and the facts provide an answer. Those suggesting abortion as a factor of any kind in this area are grasping at ancient straws.

Dr. Joseph P. Donnelly was former medical director of Margaret Hague Hospital in New Jersey. From 1947 to 1961, there were 115,000 deliveries at his maternity hospital with no abortions. Dr. Donnelly says: "Abortion is *never* necessary to save the life of the mother."

Dr. Roy S. Heffernan of Tufts University, speaking to the Congress of the American College of Surgeons, said:

> "Anyone who performs a therapeutic abortion is either ignorant of modern methods of treating the complications of pregnancy or is unwilling to take the time to use them." 94

Dr. Bernard J. Pisani, Professor of Obstetrics and Gynecology at the New York University School of Medicine said:

"Medical reasons for provoking abortion are just about non-existent. In fact, no basis on pure medical grounds ever really stands up."

Dr. John L. Grady, former Chief of Staff at Glades General Hospital in Florida, and author of the excellent book *Abortion - Yes or No?,*" has said:

"Thousands of physicians across the United States, each of whom has cared for hundreds of mothers and infants during their respective years of practice, state firmly they have never in these thousands of pregnancies seen a single instance where the life of the infant had to be sacrificed to save the mother, nor have they seen a situation where a mother has been lost for failure of the physician to perform an abortion. In fact, in more than 13 years of obstetrical practice, I never lost a mother from any cause. Moreover, during that time, at the public hospital where I was a staff member, there were thousands of babies delivered and, to my knowledge, not a single therapeutic abortion. Thus, with today's advanced medical knowledge and practice, a "therapeutic" abortion is *never* necessary, because competent physicians, using the latest medical and surgical techniques, can preserve the lives of both the mother and the child."

The "save the wife" syndrome, like every other argument of the abortionists, is based on a false premise to generate sentiment in favor of the murder of the unborn.

Murder
for
Fun £ Profit

The extent of the holocaust may be viewed in terms of a "body count" which annually surpasses traffic deaths, heart disease, and cancer - a "body count" which also historically surpasses the combined wars of America since 1775. More relevant to the continuing escalation of the death toll is the philosophical bent of the average citizen on the question of abortion.

A moral revolution has taken place in this generation which should stagger the imagination of those who purport to advocate some degree of order in society. Civilizations from bygone eras have demonstrated by their disappearance that social experimentation with the destruction of the family unit is devastating. Even atheistic Russia has abandoned such projects after sincere efforts to find a workable alternative to family life.

As we debate and address the abortion issue, we must stress this type of reasoning. Whether one is motivated by Christian beliefs or whether he is a Russian atheist who was personally involved in their experiments is immaterial. Reason demands that we not allow America to degenerate into personal anarchy, which will unquestionably destroy the nation.

We see in this country a growing *"acceptance of the unwarranted extermination of human beings as a national necessity."* This is the Nazi mentality. Certainly, the arguments put forth by proponents have their roots in superficial logic. However, in debating this subject, it is imperative that we demand some semblance of intellectual accountability. Laying aside the religious considerations as relevant only to those who believe the Bible, we may yet ask for the reasoning behind wholesale slaughter of the innocents in any civilized society.

"Murder for fun and profit" would be an excellent place to begin an inquiry. The "sex is fun" syndrome permeates every corner of society, from co-ed dormitories at both state and church supported schools to the typical comedy fare of television seven nights per week. The "fun" ends for those who discover the reality that, in American society, venereal disease is second only to the common cold in frequency among teenagers. One of every four young people in this nation will contract venereal disease before reaching age 20. By the way, for the sake of you humanists who happen to read this, venereal disease is not a religious issue; it is a physical problem which often accompanies advanced promiscuity. It occurs in those who are exercising their "right" to reject any attempts to impose Biblical morality upon society.

Sex causes babies. Not a very profound observation, perhaps, but it explains the "murder for fun" mentality. As cited in another chapter of this book, Dr. C. Everett Koop, Surgeon-in-Chief at Philadelphia's Children's Hospital, a man with a world-wide reputation in gynecology, says, "A full 97% of abortions occur for matters of convenience and economy." This is murder for fun. A decision is made by someone to have sex. A decision is further made to terminate a life not anticipated when the "fun" began. A study done for *Newsweek* magazine, published June 5, 1978, showed that of the women who have abortions, one out of five has already had an abortion; three out of four are unmarried. This is murder for fun.

Thinking has shifted in America from the once touted "Puritanically induced attitudes toward sex" to a national disregard for any kind of limitations. Under the guise of "personal liberty," we are moving toward the view that sex is a "right," no matter what the consequences. From this kind of thinking comes the "women's rights" wing of pro-abortionists.

Drawing on the 1973 U.S. Supreme Court decision, the pro-abortion feminists and their compatriots speak of "freedom of choice," "a woman's right to her own body," and "the right of privacy." Such over-simplification ignores the whole framework of societal "rights" developed over thousands of years of man's legal history. No human being has a "right" to harm himself or another human being apart from the sanction of society as a whole. As a case in point, the death penalty may only be implemented as a result of law enacted for the good of society.

A woman's right to her own body does not include drug abuse or suicide. It does not automatically legalize prostitution. Thus, the need to declare abortion a "national necessity" - for the preservation of women's rights! - for the right to privacy! - to preserve freedom of choice in the sex life of the individual! "We must learn to accept the unwarranted extermination of human beings as a national necessity!" So goes the Nazi mentality.

Any woman has the right to have sex. Any woman has a right to refrain from sexual activity. However, once conception has occurred, the rights of another human being are involved.

Under United States law, unborn children have sued and been awarded damages for injuries from accidents (Torrigan v. Watertown News Co., 352 Mass. 446). Unborn children have inherited property, qualified for social security payments, and won damages after dying in the womb by means of suits filed in their behalf (Abortion, the Practice of Medicine, and the Due Process of Law," UCLA Law Review 233, 1969). "Murder for fun" has no legal, logical, or moral leg to stand on.

"Murder for profit" is the other side of the same coin. To allow a woman and her doctor to agree to abort any baby at any stage of pregnancy is like asking the proverbial fox to guard the henhouse. Presumably, most doctors are honorable men. Without presuming anything the whole world knows there are enough dishonorable doctors to extort hundreds of millions of dollars each year in falsified and inflated Medicaid claims.

Dr. Bernard Nathanson, in his book *Aborting America* (Doubleday, 1979), tells of one of his acquaintances in the medical profession who earned $185,000 in 18 months as a *weekend* worker - a part-time employee in an abortion clinic. Any woman desiring an abortion for any reason may easily find someone who has taken the "Oath of Hypocrisy" in addition to the "Oath of Hippocrates."

In the yellow pages of the Dallas, Texas phone book, abortion clinics are listed under "Birth Control." Nineteen clinics accept this definitive listing. An investigation by the *Chicago Tribune* in 1978 found many clinics in that city operating with "doctors" who had no license to practice medicine. These people, in countless instances, were performing "abortions" on women who were not pregnant. This, of course, is not an example of "murder for profit," but the profit motive is much in evidence.

The abortion business, in America alone, will surpass one quarter of a billion dollars in 1981. Every major study since the abortion boom has shown that most candidates for abortion are not poor. Sixty-seven percent are white and most of these are upper middle class women who go to the more expensive clinics. These are not abortions for supposed physical necessity. Most abortion is birth control, pure and simple. Murder for fun and profit.

The Socio—Economic Holocaust

Toying with human life for the supposed "good of society" reaches into many areas. The more philosophical thinkers have resorted to a twisted sort of idealism.

"He who is not physically and mentally healthy and worthy must not perpetuate his misery in the body of his child."

Such a statement could be heard in discussion groups on almost any college campus in America. When abortion is the topic, social engineering inevitably raises this banner. Molders of the public mind and champions of the common good are not innovative thinkers by any means. The quotation above is from Adolph Hitler in *Mein Kampf.*

The more practical thinkers suggest the fear of overpopulation with its attendant starvation and lack of square footage for those who will have only standing room left on earth by the year ???? A.D. Somehow, in their research, they overlook the fact that every human being alive on earth today could stand comfortably in the State of North Carolina.

In the *National Catholic Register* (September 1980), Roger Revelle, former Director of the Harvard Center for Population Studies has concluded that with the use of presently known methods, the agricultural resources available on only 24% of the earth's land area are capable of feeding some 40 billion people, almost 10 times the size of the world's population. Of course, getting enough of the land away from government ownership to grow the food is another matter.

The other side of the picture is the devastation of human productivity wrought by the wholesale slaughter of the past decade. An article published by "The Atlanta Journal and Constitution" (4/23/78), entitled "Birthrate Watched for its Effect on U.S.," tells the story:

> "The present birthrate is about 1.8 children per woman. A rate of 2.1 is the minimum level at which the population replaces itself.

> "The experts are now concerned that the birthrate will remain too low. They say it is vital to the nation's growth that current birth goals be realized.

> "Those producing children tend to be less suited to contribute to society and tend to be poor parents.

> "The tax base may decrease because there will be fewer high-salaried wage earners in the population.

> "The proportion of Americans aged 65 and older will increase, thus putting an even heavier tax burden on future generations to support the elderly."

Three-fourths of the tillable land on earth has never been used for a food crop of any kind. Seventeen nations surpass America in the production of food per acre. If anything, the solution to world hunger problems lies in bringing enough babies into the world to till the soil and discover better production methods.

The "Sun Belt" states are experiencing unparalleled growth and prosperity. The northern states are declining. Most experts attribute this trend to shifting population factors. Industry moves toward a younger population with a broader tax base where people work and produce and reproduce to supply a continual labor force. Murdering 1½ million citizens annually is not the answer to social and economic difficulties.

"The Population Slow-Down - A Challenge to the Military," by Col. Robert K. de Marcellus raises another point worthy of note. He suggests that the U.S. defense posture at home and abroad will seriously decline due to the rapid drop in man-power and the decrease of national defense expenditures in favor of sustaining a disproportionately aged population.

Of course the economy and national defense pale into insignificance as we view the devastating effect of abortion on the attitudes and aspirations of the "movers and shakers" of the scientific world. As reported in *Newsweek* (9/20/76), Dr. Bentley Glass delivered a presidential address to the American Association for the Advancement of Science. As a geneticist, he looked ahead to the day when the government will *require* what science has made possible, and I quote:

> "No parents will, in that future time, have a right to burden society with a malformed or a mentally incompetent child."
>
> **Dr. Bentley Glass**
> **Presidential Address**
> **American Association for the**
> **Advancement of Science**
>
> "He who is not physically and mentally healthy and worthy must not perpetuate his misery in the body of his child."
>
> **Adolph Hitler**
> *Mein Kampf*

In the same issue of *Newsweek*, Dr. Leon Kass, the renowned University of Chicago biologist, viewed the scenery in this fashion:

> "We have paid some high prices for the technological conquest of nature, but

111

none so high as the intellectual and spiritual costs of seeing nature as mere material for our manipulation. And clearly, if we come to see ourselves as meat, then meat we shall become."

In response, noted *Newsweek* columnist George F. Will made this comment:

"Politics has paved the way for this degradation. *Meat we have already become,* at Ypres and Verdun, Dresden and Hiroshima, Auschwitz and the Gulag. Is it a coincidence that this century . . . also is the dawn of the abortion age?"

Imagine the audacity of a respected columnist for *Newsweek* suggesting a connection between the Nazi mentality of Auschwitz and the abortionist mentality of America! Buried somewhere deep in his genes may lurk the remnants of a redneck fundamentalist heritage, undetected by amniocentesis.

The Population Explosion Myth

By Dennis L. Cuddy, Ph. D.

*Reprinted from National Pro-Life Journal

Today we constantly hear about the suffering people of an overly crowded India. While there is little doubt that many people in India do suffer from a lack of food, this is not necessarily because of the number of people inhabiting that vast land. India has less people per square mile than England, West Germany or Taiwan (India - 508 per square mile, England - 592, West Germany - 643, Taiwan - 1181). There is actually not a "population problem" as such today, as all the people of the world could fit side-by-side into Greater Jacksonville, Florida. What we do have is a problem of food distribution and the availability of natural resources.

Nick Eberstadt of Harvard's Center for Population Studies found that the world's population growth peaked at 1.9% around 1970 and is now down to 1.7%. In western Europe the growth rate has dropped 50%, in North America 30%, in China 30%, and in India 10%. Interestingly, demographer Donald Bogue in a Population Reference Bureau paper estimated that only 4.7% of the decline in the world fertility rate could be attributed to family planning efforts. Currently, the U.S. fertility rate is 1.7 (a rate of 2.1 is necessary merely to maintain a population replacement level). And the decline in fertility in this country is most pronounced among blacks, American Indians and Mexican-Americans (25% of native American women have been sterilized with monies earmarked by treaty agreements for medical needs, and 35% of all Puerto Rican women have been sterilized).

What this dramatic decline in the fertility rate means is that in the not too distant future, there will be a disproportionate number of elderly compared to the number of youth. Because this will place a tremendous economic burden upon the non-elderly to care for our older citizens, there will be a growing advocacy of euthanasia. Indeed, Dr. Christian Barnard (of heart transplant fame) has suggested that doctors begin to practice "active euthanasia" now. When asked about the ethics of his suggestion, Barnard replied with chilling logic: "You have already agreed to destroy a life (through abortion) the quality of which you don't even know, yet you say you can't act to destroy a life, the quality of which you know has disappeared."

Many of the problems we face today regarding the increasing disrespect for human life originated with the knee-jerk reaction to what was described as a population crisis. Nearly two centuries ago, Thomas Malthus developed the theory that population grows geometrically while food production grows arithmetically. However, his theory underestimated the increasingly effective utilization of natural resources and new methods of increasing food production.

In addition, there has always been a problem with the use of statistics to analyze the supposed "population crisis." For if one took the 1936 U.S. birthrate (18.4 per 1000 people) and compared it to the 1957 rate (25.3), one could project that this country would have 400 million people by the year 2000, which is an absurdity. Then, if one took the 1957 rate (25.3) and compared it to the 1975 rate (14.9), one could project that the last baby in this country would be born in 1992 - another absurdity!

Though the promoters of the "population bomb" theory have realized the questionable use of statistics to prove their theory, they have proceeded nonstop with all available means (e.g. advocacy of contraception. abortion, sterilization, homosexual rights, a "do your own thing" mentality, and a humanistic disbelief in God) to diffuse this "bomb."

The Rockefellers, for example, have been prominent in the population-control movement through their financial support of various organizations and their influence on numerous foundations and commissions. In a LOOK magazine, Feb. 9, 1965 article, John D. Rockefeller III said: "The choice is no longer whether population stabilization is necessary but only how and when it can be achieved . . . The population problem is so ramified that only Government can attack it on the scale required."

But the solutions proposed by such "social engineers" are unnecessary, as Dr. Jonas Salk cautions us to look at the population cycle of fruit flies: "Their populations start shooting up in what appears to be an exponential manner, but then reaches a 'point of inflection' and levels off instead."

Zero Population Growth (which sends condoms with their Valentine's Day cards) is another prominent group within the population-control movement, and the results of their "population crisis" promotions were recently evidenced in a SCIENCE DIGEST article. The article described how New York's ZPG had conducted a contest for teens to write solutions to the "population crisis," and the teen's essays included such solutions as "suicide, legalized murder, and even cannibalism."

Perhaps the leading force in population-control, however, is Planned Parenthood. Its Margaret Sanger advocated situational ethics and birth control "to create a race of thoroughbreds" (BIRTH CONTROL REVIEW, Nov. 1921). This forerunner of Hitler's eugenics movement also proclaimed that "the most merciful thing that the large family does to one of its infant members is to kill it." (WOMEN AND THE NEW RACE).

Today, Planned Parenthood does not use such forceful language, but rather more subtle terms, like advocating the need for "genetic counseling." Concerning such "counseling," one finds that for every black who has Sickle-cell anemia, there are 40 "carriers." Thus, to "counsel" these individuals not to have any children would almost amount to "counseling" genocide against the black race. Then, what about Tay-Sach which largely affects Jews? Furthermore, each one of us has 3 - 4 "defective" genes, which may result in a cleft chin or something more serious. How would we be "counseled?"

It is enlightening to know that Planned Parenthood's five-year (1976-80) plan of developing and delivering sex education programs to "modify attitudes and change behavior" was largely successful, as were its efforts to remove parental consent laws. Even more revealing are the following quotations from a special supplement to FAMILY PLANNING PERSPECTIVES by Planned Parenthood-World Population entitled, "Examples of Proposed Measures to Reduce U.S. Fertility, by Universality or Selectivity of Impact:"

1) Universal Impact-restructure family, encourage increased homosexuality, educate for family limitation, fertility control agents in the water supply, encourage women to work.*

2) Economic Impact - tax policies: marriage tax, child tax, additional on parents with more than one or two children in school.

3) Social Impact - compulsory sterilization of all who have two children except for a few who would be allowed three, confine childbearing to a limited number of adults, stock certificate type permits for children, discouragement of private home ownership, stop awarding public housing on the basis of family size.

4) Measures Predicted on Existing Motivations - payment to encourage sterilization, abortion and contraception, along with allowing certain contraceptives to be distributed non-medically.

It would seem that the mentality of George Orwell's book, "1984" is already here. We must wake up before it is too late, and inform the public that the real danger we face in the future is a population "implosion," not "explosion." The social engineers of Planned Parenthood must be exposed for what they are and what they are trying to do; then the people will realize that the eugenics movement did not die with Adolf Hitler.

*Dr. Peter Bourne, dismissed from the Carter administration for improperly prescribing drugs, is now with the U.N. as a consultant on the world's water needs.

*This chapter first appeared as an article in the National Pro-Life Journal, an excellent quarterly publication, and is reprinted with premission of both the author and the journal.

National Pro-Life Journal
P.O. Box 172
Fairfax, Virginia 22030
—Subscription Rates—
1 Year-$5   2 Years-$8.50   3 Years-$10

A Personal Testimony

By Elizabeth Kelly

It all started a little over ten years ago. Summer was rapidly drawing to a close. Soon our six-year old boy would enter the first grade and our five-year old daughter would begin kindergarten. Now I would have a lot of free time on my hands, and I was considering going back to school. It would be difficult, but I was excited at the prospect of getting a degree and embarking on a career.

Life was wonderful. I had a good husband, two fine children, a boy and a girl - the perfect family, I thought. Now, at 27, I could concentrate on some things I had been wanting to do with my life.

But things do not always go as planned. Suddenly my circumstances completely

125

reversed. I didn't feel well any more. I was very tired from early morning to late afternoon. Then I began to think. Could it be possible? Yes. I thought it not only could be, but was. I was going to have a baby.

Joy flooded my heart - followed suddenly by fear. My mind raced back seven years. There I was, living in a strange town, 20 years old and expecting my first child. I was sitting outside a hospital lab waiting for a technician to return with the results of a blood test. As I nervously waited in a chilly corridor, she returned. "You are a rare one indeed," she said laughingly. "You're O-negative."

"Oh, no!" I thought. "My husband's blood type is positive. That's a combination which causes blood problems, transfusions and sometimes death of babies." As I mentioned these things, she attempted to console me by saying that problems seldom occur until your third child. In the seven years which followed I began to have serious health problems of unexplained origin, and now my third child was growing daily in my womb.

As the days went by, I began having unusual difficulty. I reached my second

126

month and thought I should visit a gynecologist. Surely he would be able to give me something that would help me. I had already lost five pounds. His idea of help wasn't exactly what I had in mind. After discussing the blood problems and general state of my health, he suggested an abortion. Yes, he thought I should kill my unborn baby. On another visit I was told that my baby would likely be deformed or retarded. About the third month, I began running an elevated temperature, often 102 or 103 degrees. Day and night I was in pain. Sometimes it was almost unbearable, and I was hardly able to keep anything on my stomach. (Five years and six doctors later, my ailment was diagnosed as Crohn's disease, a very rare gastrointestinal disorder.) On another visit I was reminded that I could have an abortion. My earliest recollections of the word "abortion" was that it meant murdering the most innocent, helpless form of life. In those days the word "abortion" was seldom used and, then, usually whispered.

At five months, the baby moved, tiny little flutters confirming the presence of a precious life. Even though I had gained no weight, I was beginning to be visibly pregnant.

Daily, my condition worsened. Every growing pressure from the baby intensified the problem and often I spent 18 to 20 hours a day in bed; sometimes I couldn't get up at all. Why didn't I call my doctor? He would only repeat his best suggestion - the murder of my child.

At 7½ months I entered the hospital. There I was given I.V. feedings and treatment. Through several subsequent hospital visits I was never sorry for a moment that I hadn't had an abortion, even though the words "deformed" or "retarded" flashed through my mind quite frequently.

Time passed rather slowly for me, but finally it was spring. I knew it couldn't be much longer. Then on a beautiful morning in late April, I began to realize my time was at hand. With labor pains five minutes apart, I awakened my husband, and asked him to take me to the hospital. Tears streamed down my face as we drove the three miles. I knew that soon I would be holding my baby; and deformed, retarded, or not, I loved him.

At ll:37 that morning, a baby was born. No, he was not deformed or retarded. Today he is nine years old and a fourth grade student, a blond-haired, blue-eyed boy, perfectly normal in every way.

Neither he nor I have forgotten that the God who gives life knows best. How thankful I am for the Word of God which taught me the solemn right of every child to live - whatever his condition.

Abortion is not the answer to human suffering. Doctors such as those who suggested an abortion for me are the means of robbing countless mothers of their joy and countless children such as my son, Kasey, of their very lives.

Chronology of the New Human Life

1. Immediately upon fertilization, cellular development begins. Before implantation the sex of the new life can be determined.

2. At implantation, the new life is composed of hundreds of cells and has developed a protective hormone to prevent the mother's body from rejecting it as a foreign tissue.

3. At 17 days, the new life has developed its own blood cells; the placenta is a part of the new life and not of the mother.

4. At 18 days, occasional pulsations of a muscle - this will be the heart.

5.   At 19 days, the eyes start to develop.

6.   At 20 days, the foundation of the entire nervous system has been laid down.

7.   At 24 days, the heart has regular beats or pulsations. (This is a legal sign of life.)

8.   At 28 days, 40 pairs of muscles are developed along the trunk of the new life; arms and legs forming.

9.   At 30 days, regular blood flow within the vascular system; the ears and nasal development have begun.

10. At 40 days, the heart energy output is reported to be almost 20% of an adult.

11. At 42 days, skeleton complete and the reflexes are present.

12. At 43 days, electrical brain wave patterns can be recorded. This is usually ample evidence that "thinking" is taking place in the brain. The new life may be thought of as a thinking person.

13. At 49 days, the appearance of a miniature doll with complete fingers, toes and ears.

14. NAME CHANGED FROM EMBRYO TO FETUS. At 56 days all organs functioning - stomach, liver, kidney, brain - all systems intact. Lines in palms. All future development of new life is simply that of refinement and increase in size until maturity at approximately age 23 years. This is approximately two months before "quickening" yet there is a new life with all of its parts needing only nourishment. The mother will usually not feel the child's movements until four months after conception.

15. 9th & 10th week, squints, swallows, retracts tongue.

16. 11th & 12th week, arms & legs move, sucks thumb, inhales and exhales amniotic fluid, nails appearing.

17. 16 weeks (four months), genital organs clearly differentiated, grasps with hands, swims, kicks and turns

somersaults (STILL NOT FELT BY MOTHER).

18. 18 weeks, vocal cords working ... can cry.

19. 20 weeks, hair appears on head; weight - one pound; height - 12 inches.

The Bible and Abortion

"The Lord gave her conception . . . "
Ruth 4:13

"The Lord had shut up her womb."
I Samuel 1:5

For those who believe the Bible the subject of abortion is a study in simplicity. As indicated clearly by the scripture portions cited above, God is the Author of life. There are no accidental conceptions in a world overseen by a Sovereign God who both shuts up the womb and gives conception according to His divine purpose.

Moses and Aaron were children of incest (Exodus 6:20) yet they grew up to become the spiritual and political liberators of an entire nation.

137

Solomon was a child of adultery (II Samuel 12:24) but the Bible says, "The Lord loved him," and he grew into the richest, wisest, and most honored king of all the ages.

Rahab the harlot had a crucial place in the lineage of the Lord Jesus Christ. (Matthew 1:5)

Speaking of a man blind from his birth, the Lord said:

"Neither hath this man sinned, nor his parents - but that the works of God should be made manifest in him." (John 9:3)

Ecclesiastes 11:5 says:

"As thou knowest not . . . how the bones do grow in the womb of her that is with child: even so thou knowest not the works of God who maketh all."

The full impact of the anti-Christian nature of abortion may be felt by taking a mental journey back in time. Using modern guidelines, the Department of Human Resources in Nazareth would most certainly have provided counseling to a girl named

Mary. Her youth, her poverty, and her pregnancy out of wedlock would have made her the perfect candidate. The decree from Caesar Augustus that all the world should be taxed would have provided the funds. The taxpayers, the politicians, and the Humanist Gestapo would have combined in a socially acceptable effort to abort the Saviour of the world!

To declare that an abortion is anything less than murder is to deny the obvious for those who take the Bible at face value. To abort the Lord Jesus Christ or any other living soul in the first trimester is, in the minds of some, nothing more than the removal of tissue. How much more ludicrous this is when those who advocate such thinking claim to be religious leaders and ministers of the Word of God.

Should any such "men of the cloth" crawl out from under a rock long enough to read this chapter, I say to you what the Lord Jesus Christ said to the apostate preachers of His day - "Ye serpents, ye generation of vipers - how shall ye escape the damnation of Hell!"

The Psalmist David said concerning his birth:

> "Thine eyes did see my substance, yet being unperfect: and in thy book all my members were written, which in continuance were fashioned, when as yet there was none of them."
>
> Psalm 139:16

God knew the reality of David as a living soul before he ever came into being.

To the prophet Jeremiah God said:

> "Before I formed thee in the belly I knew thee; and before thou camest forth out of the womb I sanctified thee, and I ordained thee a prophet unto the nations."
>
> Jeremiah 1:5

Many other scriptures could be cited to prove that every life is a gift from God, and only those who attempt to play God tamper with a life.

For those who believe the Bible, God only needs to say something one time to establish it as truth. Repetition is pointless for those "humanists in sheep's clothing," masquerading as preachers of a Bible they do not believe.

In the meantime, those of us who believe the Word of God must be willing to lift up a standard against "Abortion - The American Holocaust." To sin by complicity or by silence, as 1.5 million souls for whom Christ died are murdered each year, is inexcusable.

Back in the days when justice still lived in the legal systems of America, an accessory to murder was as severely punished as the murderer himself. Justice is still coming some day, and "the Judge of all the earth" will do right as He deals with those who advocate the slaughter of the innocents in the name of God and the Bible.

God said in Jeremiah 19:

"Behold, I will bring evil upon this place, the which whosoever heareth, his ears shall tingle. Because they have forsaken me . . . and have filled this place with *THE BLOOD OF INNOCENTS."*

The Lord Jesus said in Luke 24 that only a fool is even slow of heart to believe *all* that the prophets have spoken. Believe it or not, this nation is begging for the judgment of God is we allow "Abortion - The American Holocaust" to continue unchecked and unchallenged. **141**

STATE OF NORTH CAROLINA

V S

CHRISTIAN LIBERTY

Foreword by Senator Jesse Helms

Read first-hand the story of the trial and Christian School controversy in North Carolina.

This effort by the Christian schools of North Carolina resulted in a new law, termed by Attorney William Ball "The Magna Carta of religious liberty for the nation."

Kent Kelly